MW01628362

Written by Ryan Jaroncyk

Illustrated by Lisa Sodera

Published and distributed by
Creation Book Publishers

www.creationbookpublishers.com

ISBN: 978-0-949906-70-0

Cover design, layout and illustrations by Lisa Sodera at

onesmallmango.com

Printed: March 2008

For information on this book or on creation/evolution issues, contact:

CreationOnTheWeb.com

Notes for parents

Newspapers, magazines, television programs, books, and schools constantly present children with an evolutionary perspective of the natural world. *The Adventures of Arkie the Archaeopteryx* aims to inspire young children to view the natural world through a biblical lens. In this book, the title character is an archaeopteryx, an extinct bird with features that some have said 'proves' it shared a common ancestor with reptiles.

Dr Vij Sodera, in his book *One Small Speck to Man ~ the evolution myth*, says:

> "It is possible for one creature to have a head and teeth that completely resemble another creature, yet for it not to have any relationship ancestral or descendant to the second creature. So if these principles are applied to the claws of the hoatzin and turaco, then this demonstrates simply and only that living birds that have claws on their front limbs exist—nothing more. And the claws, teeth, tail, and breastbone of the archaeopteryx demonstrate simply and only that creatures with such features once lived and are now extinct.
>
> "What exactly is a bird? It is important to remember that the classification of a bird (or any other class of animal for that matter) is to some significant extent an artificial label, which can act in the mind so as to impose some limit on what can be accepted or understood as a particular creature type."

Based on this logic, shared features, such as hand-like fins in a fish or teeth in a bird, can just as easily be interpreted as evidence for a common designer as they can be for a common ancestor. Join Arkie the archaeopteryx as he journeys through God's creation and meets an array of strange animals that share many weird and wonderful traits.

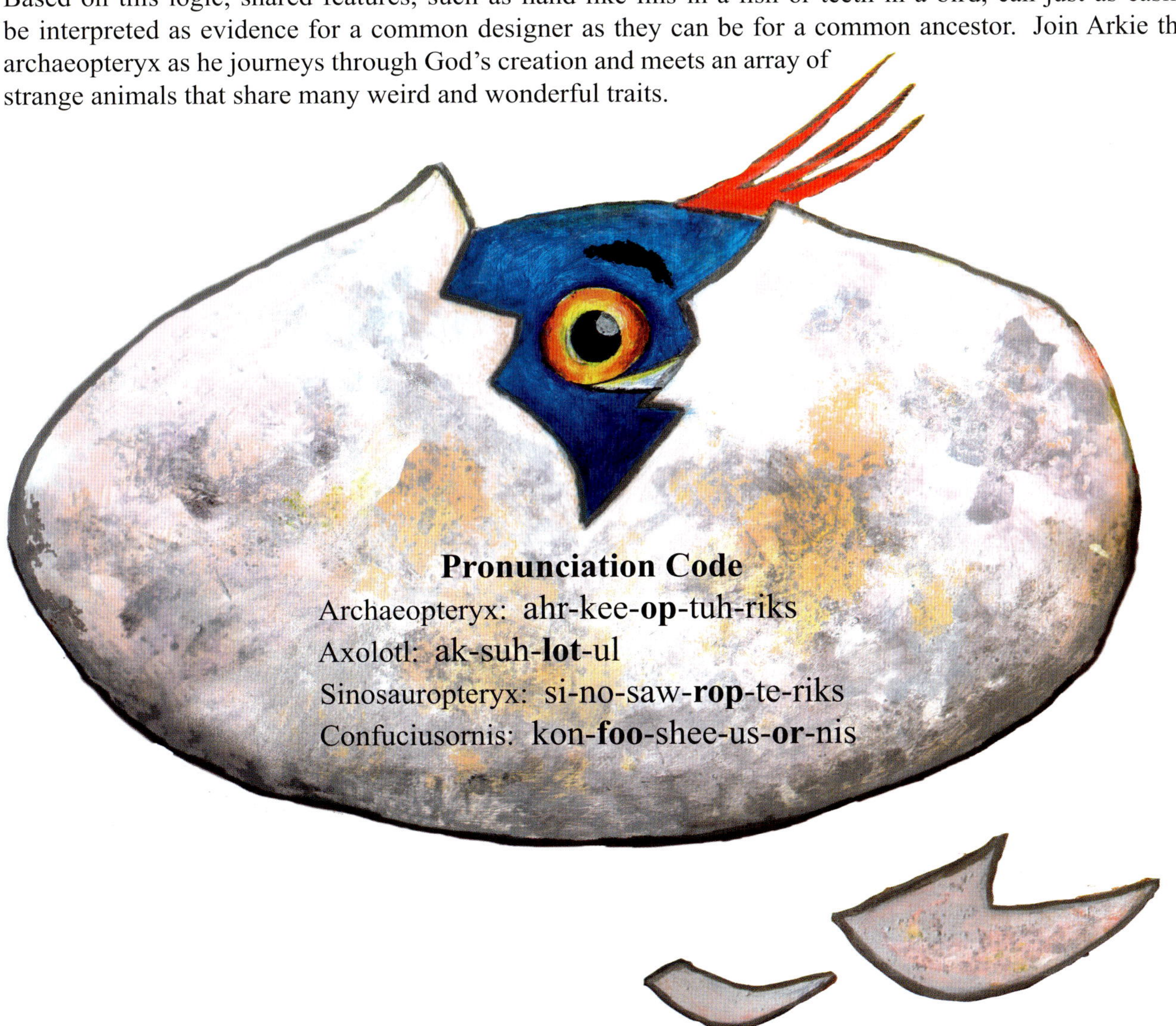

Pronunciation Code

Archaeopteryx: ahr-kee-**op**-tuh-riks
Axolotl: ak-suh-**lot**-ul
Sinosauropteryx: si-no-saw-**rop**-te-riks
Confuciusornis: kon-**foo**-shee-us-**or**-nis

About six thousand years ago, a bird hatched and his name was Arkie the archaeopteryx.

He was a very different kind of bird.

Unlike most birds,
Arkie had teeth,
claws on his wings,
and a long, bony tail.

In fact, he looked a little bit like a small dinosaur.

Arkie lived with his parents in the woods, but he longed to explore the nearby jungle. He just had to know what was out there.

After a good night's sleep, Arkie got up his courage and asked his mother if he could fly to the jungle.

“Mama, what’s over there in the jungle?” asked Arkie.

“It’s a beautiful place, with lots of animals, and trees, and flowers,” she replied.

"Can I go check it out, Mama?" he asked.

"Of course you can, Arkie. Have a good time!"

“Okay Mama, I will.
I can’t wait to see what it’s like.”

When he finally made it, he saw a whole new world. The jungle was full of amazing trees, flowers, and all different kinds of animals that he had never seen before.

After a while, Arkie became very thirsty. As he began to drink some water at the edge of a pond, a fish swam to the surface and walked toward him.

"Hello, my name is Hank the handfish."

"Wait a second! You're not a fish! Fish don't walk!" exclaimed Arkie.

"But I really *am* a fish! Didn't you know that some fish can walk underwater and on dry land at times?" replied Hank.

"I had no idea that fish could walk," said Arkie.

"I'm a special kind of fish. By the way, I didn't catch your name."

"Oh, my name is Arkie the archaeopteryx."

"What type of creature are you?" asked Hank.

"I'm a rare type of bird, and this is my first day here in the jungle."

"Nice to meet you Arkie. I have to walk back into the water so I can breathe. See you around!"

When Hank the handfish walked into the water, he swam away in an instant. Suddenly, another strange creature crawled out of the pond.

"Hello, my name is Arkie the archaeopteryx."

"My name is Laura the lobster. It's nice to meet you."

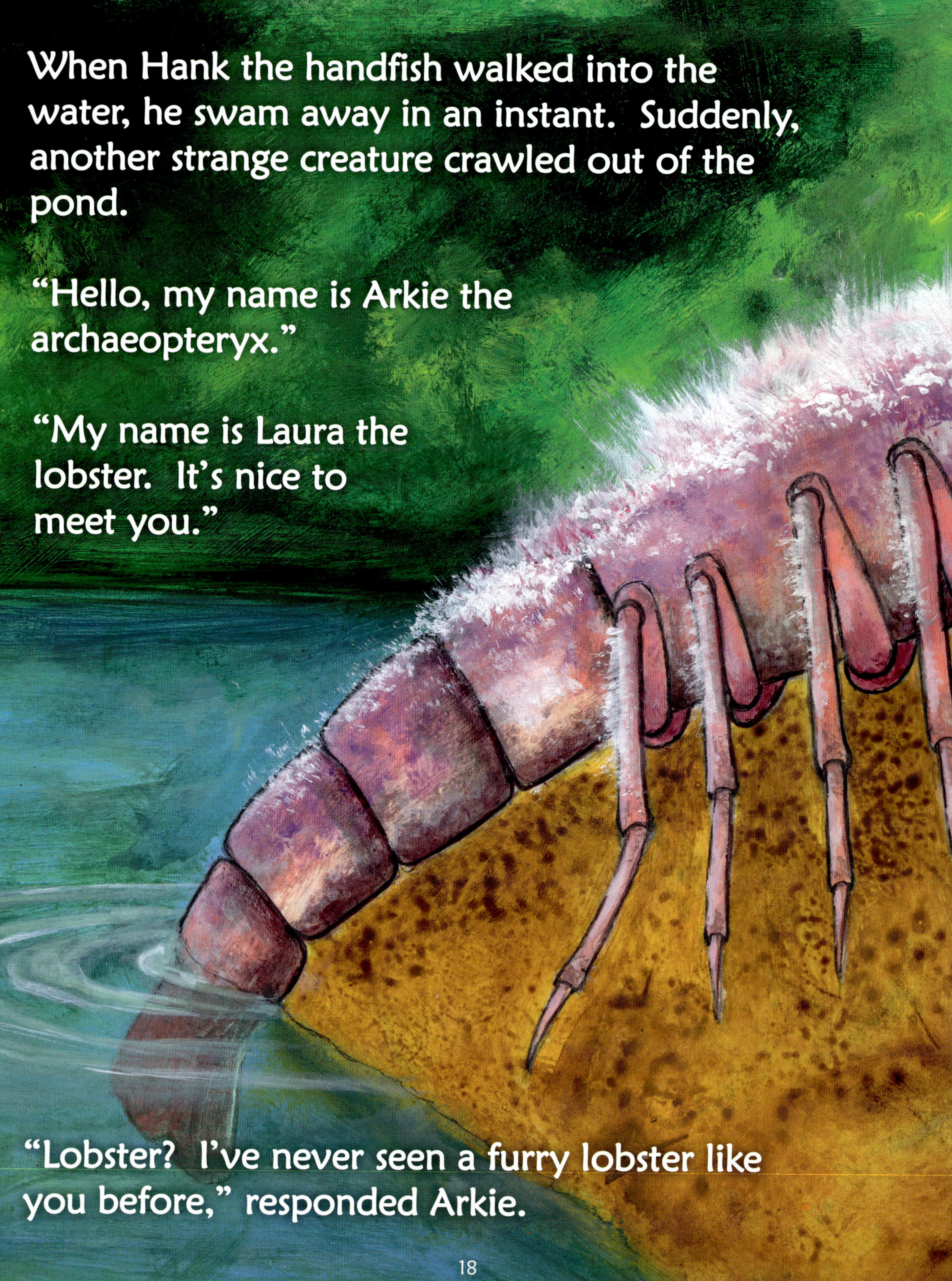

"Lobster? I've never seen a furry lobster like you before," responded Arkie.

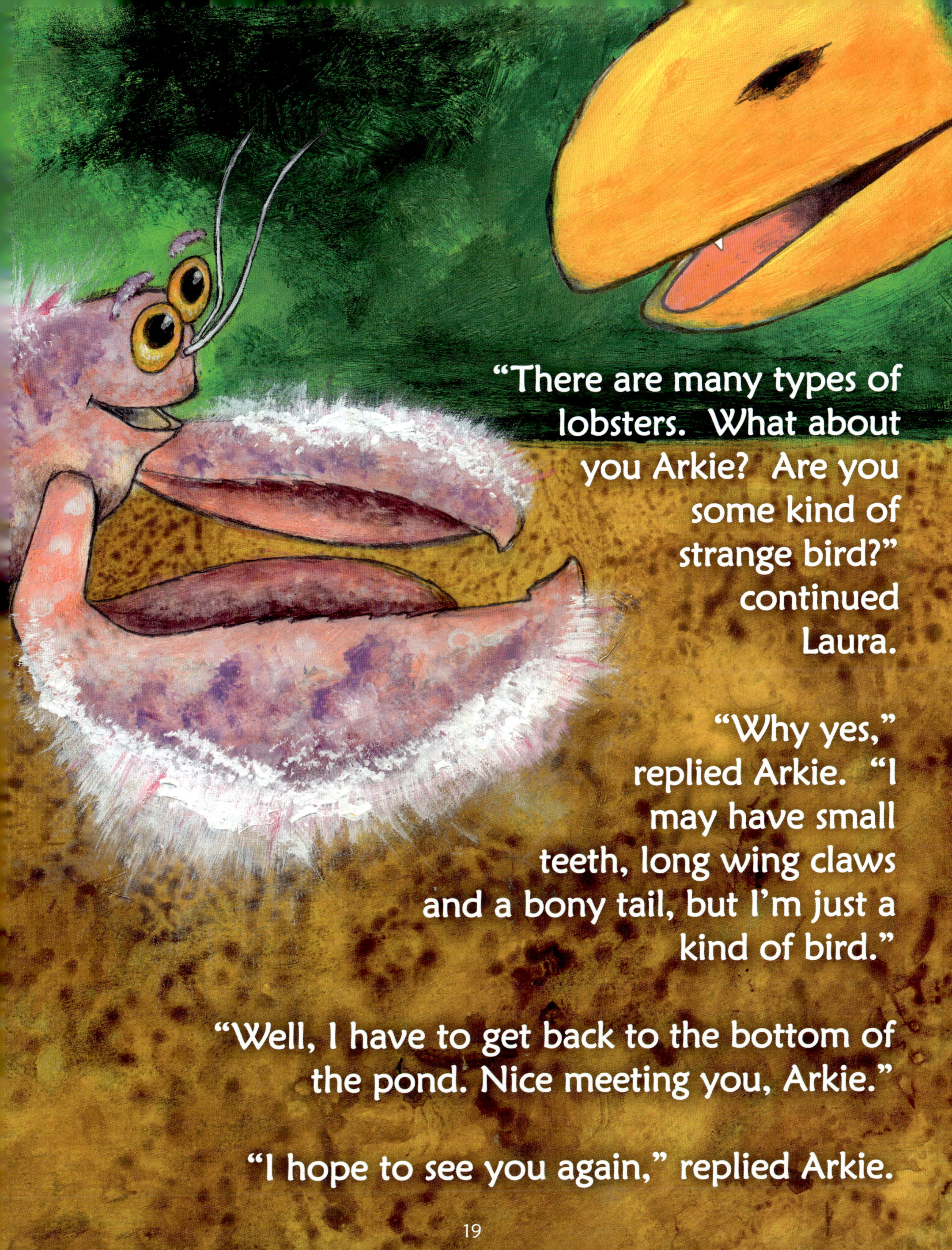

"There are many types of lobsters. What about you Arkie? Are you some kind of strange bird?" continued Laura.

"Why yes," replied Arkie. "I may have small teeth, long wing claws and a bony tail, but I'm just a kind of bird."

"Well, I have to get back to the bottom of the pond. Nice meeting you, Arkie."

"I hope to see you again," replied Arkie.

Arkie flew
into a nearby
bush to look around.

He saw what looked like another walking fish feeding in the shallow water.

He flew to the top of a floating log where he could get a better view.

"Hi, my name is Arkie the archaeopteryx. Are you a handfish too?"

"Why, I'm not a fish at all.
My name is Alex the axolotl."

"But you have gills and fins like a fish."

"Yes, but I'm not a fish. I'm just a unique amphibian."

Just then,
something
jumped onto the log.

Arkie was startled, but he kept his balance.

"Arkie, this is Freddy the frog," said Alex.

"Nice to meet you Freddy. What are those things on your back?"

"During some times of the year, I grow these hair-like fibers over parts of my body."

"So you're a hairy frog?" asked Arkie.

"That's right. Well, I've got to meet some friends. See ya."

"And I've got to swim to the bottom," said Alex.

"Wait, don't leave!" cried Arkie, but it was too late. They swam away in the blink of an eye.

It was getting hot. Arkie decided to fly up and rest in the cool shade of the jungle canopy. Suddenly, he noticed what he thought was a snake wriggling on the ground. He flew back down to meet it.

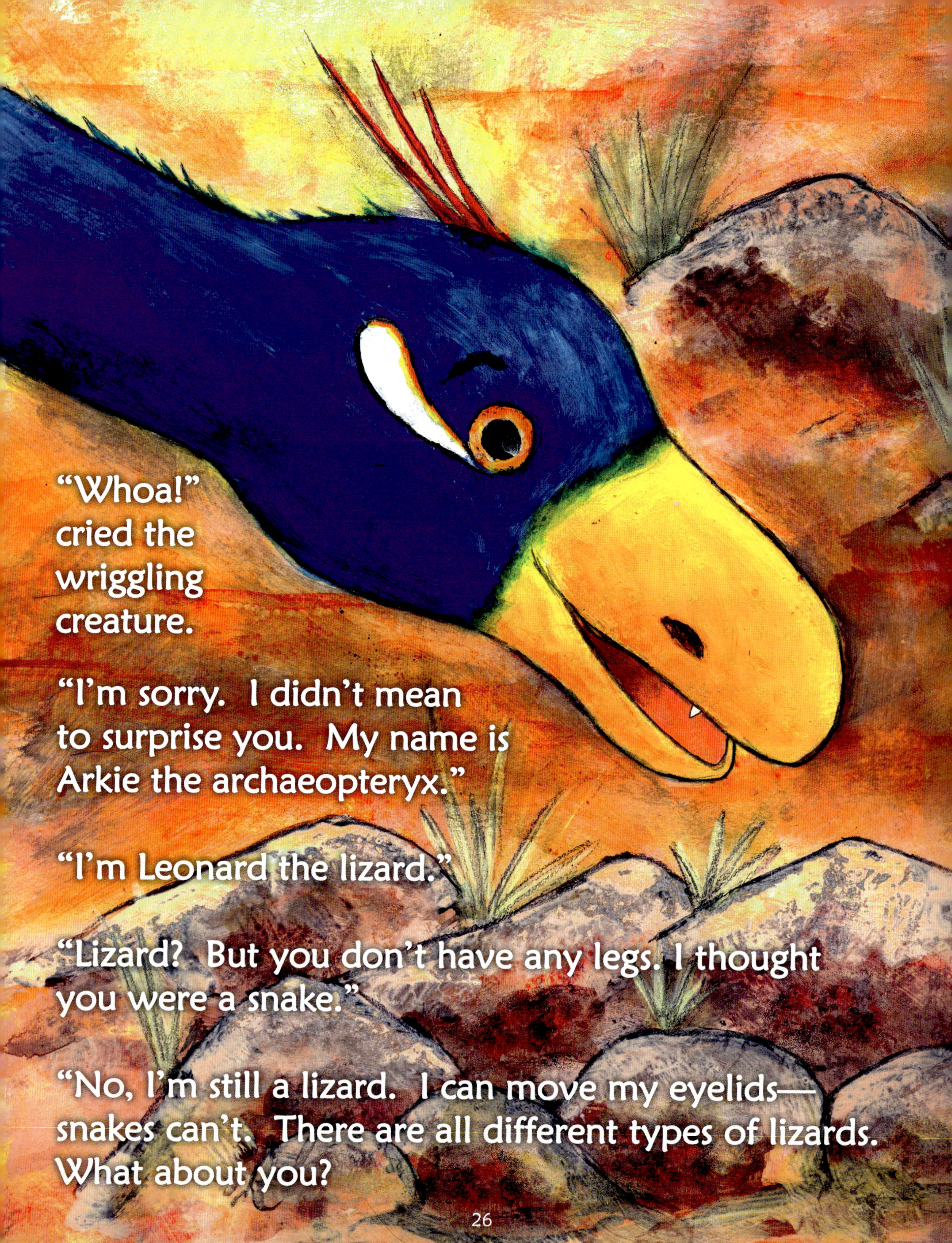

“Whoa!” cried the wriggling creature.

“I’m sorry. I didn’t mean to surprise you. My name is Arkie the archaeopteryx.”

“I’m Leonard the lizard.”

“Lizard? But you don’t have any legs. I thought you were a snake.”

“No, I’m still a lizard. I can move my eyelids—snakes can’t. There are all different types of lizards. What about you?

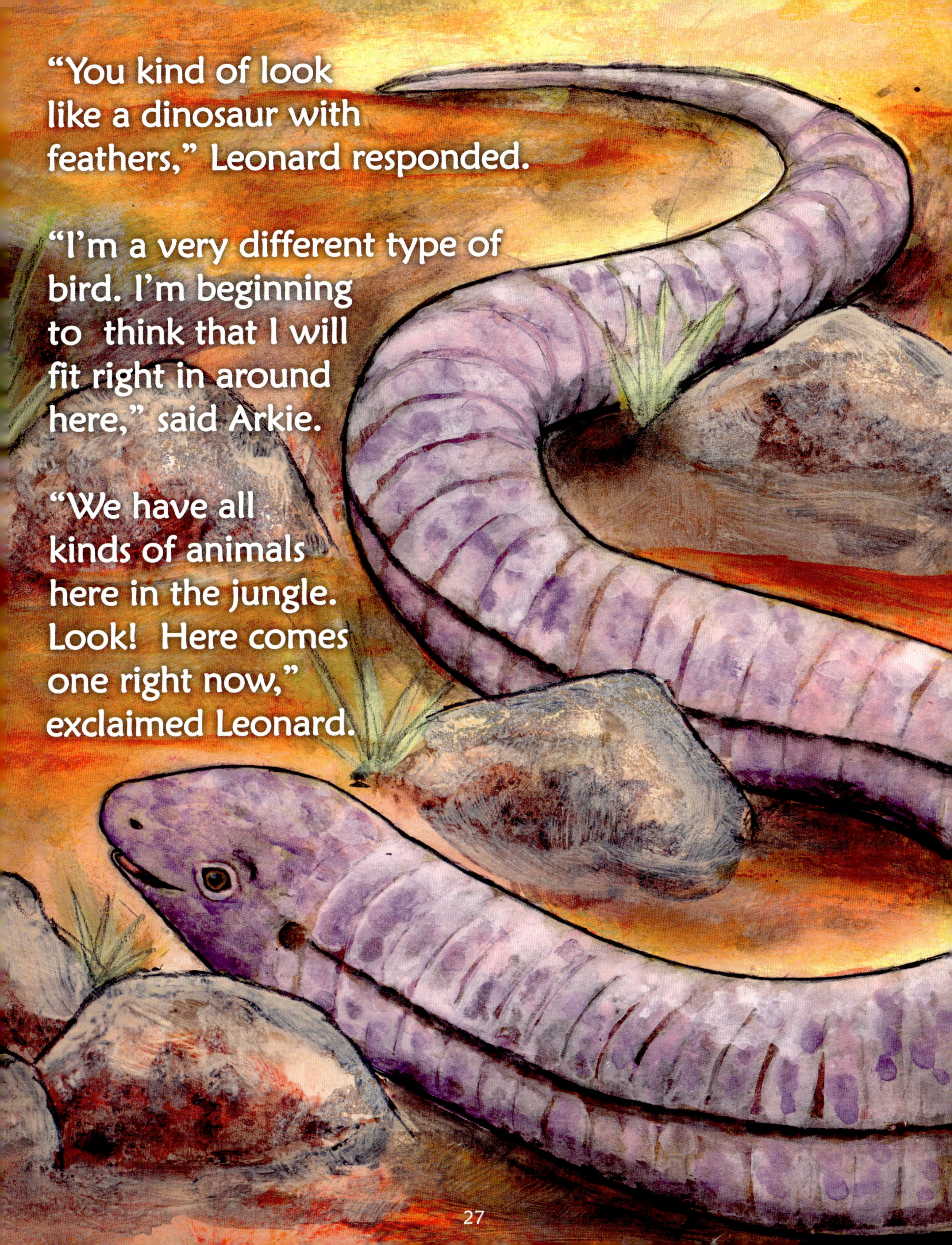

"You kind of look like a dinosaur with feathers," Leonard responded.

"I'm a very different type of bird. I'm beginning to think that I will fit right in around here," said Arkie.

"We have all kinds of animals here in the jungle. Look! Here comes one right now," exclaimed Leonard.

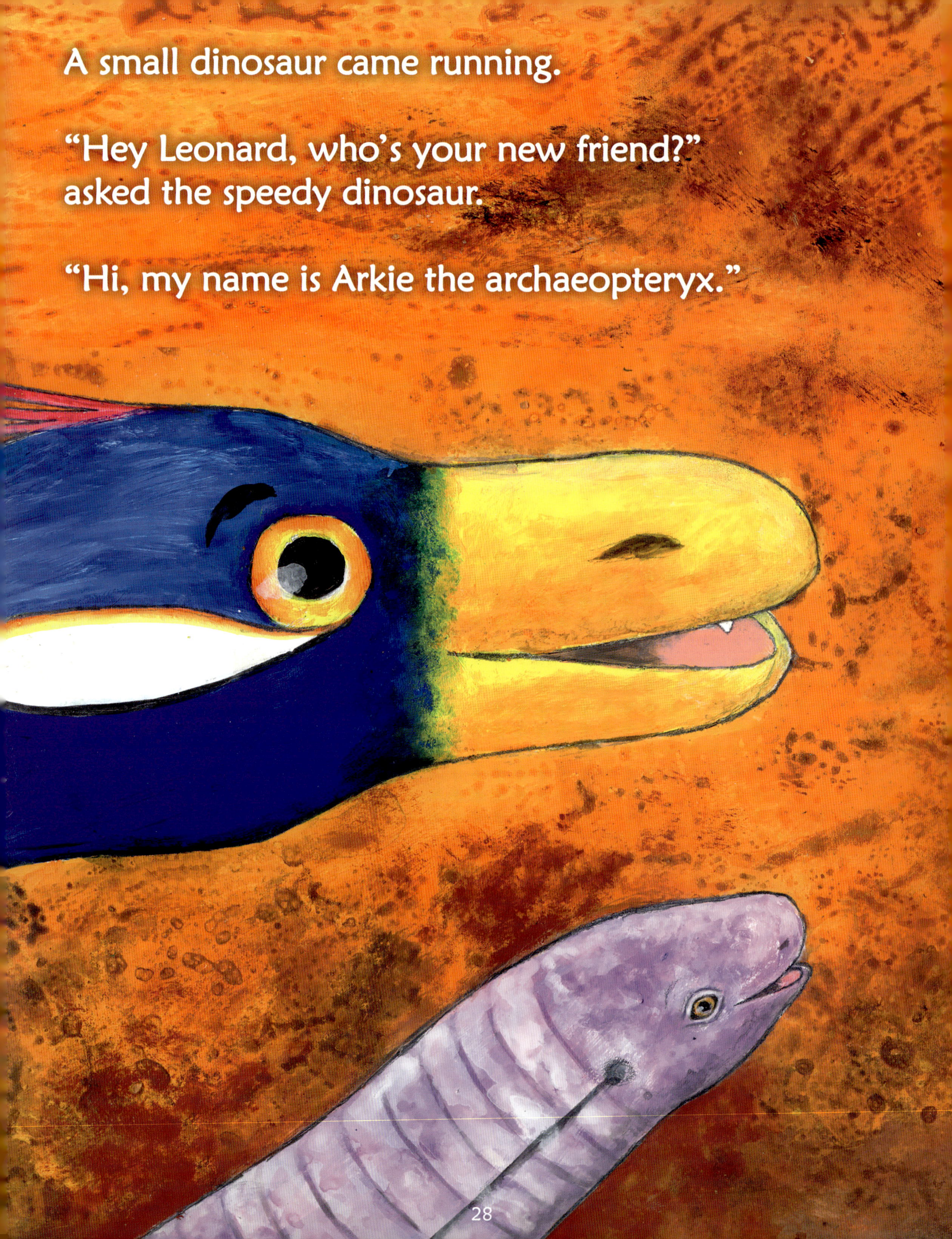

A small dinosaur came running.

"Hey Leonard, who's your new friend?" asked the speedy dinosaur.

"Hi, my name is Arkie the archaeopteryx."

"My name is Sino the sinosauropteryx. I've never seen a bird like you before."

"And you're the first dinosaur I've seen with fuzz on the back of its body."

"It's not fuzz. It's just scaly skin. Well, I'm getting hungry. I have to go now.
See you around Arkie. Bye, Leonard."

"Nice to meet you, Sino," answered Arkie.

"Bye Sino," said Leonard.

Arkie couldn't believe all the strange creatures in the jungle.

As he
was walking on
the ground, he noticed an
animal by a tall mound of dirt.

The animal had four legs and a covering of overlapping scales.

Arkie asked, “Excuse me, do you mind if I ask you a question?”

“No not at all, I’m just walking home.”

"My name is Arkie the archaeopteryx.
What type of animal are you?"

"I'm Peter the pangolin. It may seem odd, but I'm a scaly mammal. It was nice to meet you Arkie, but I have to go now. I'm tired and it's getting dark."

"Oh, okay. See you around, Peter."

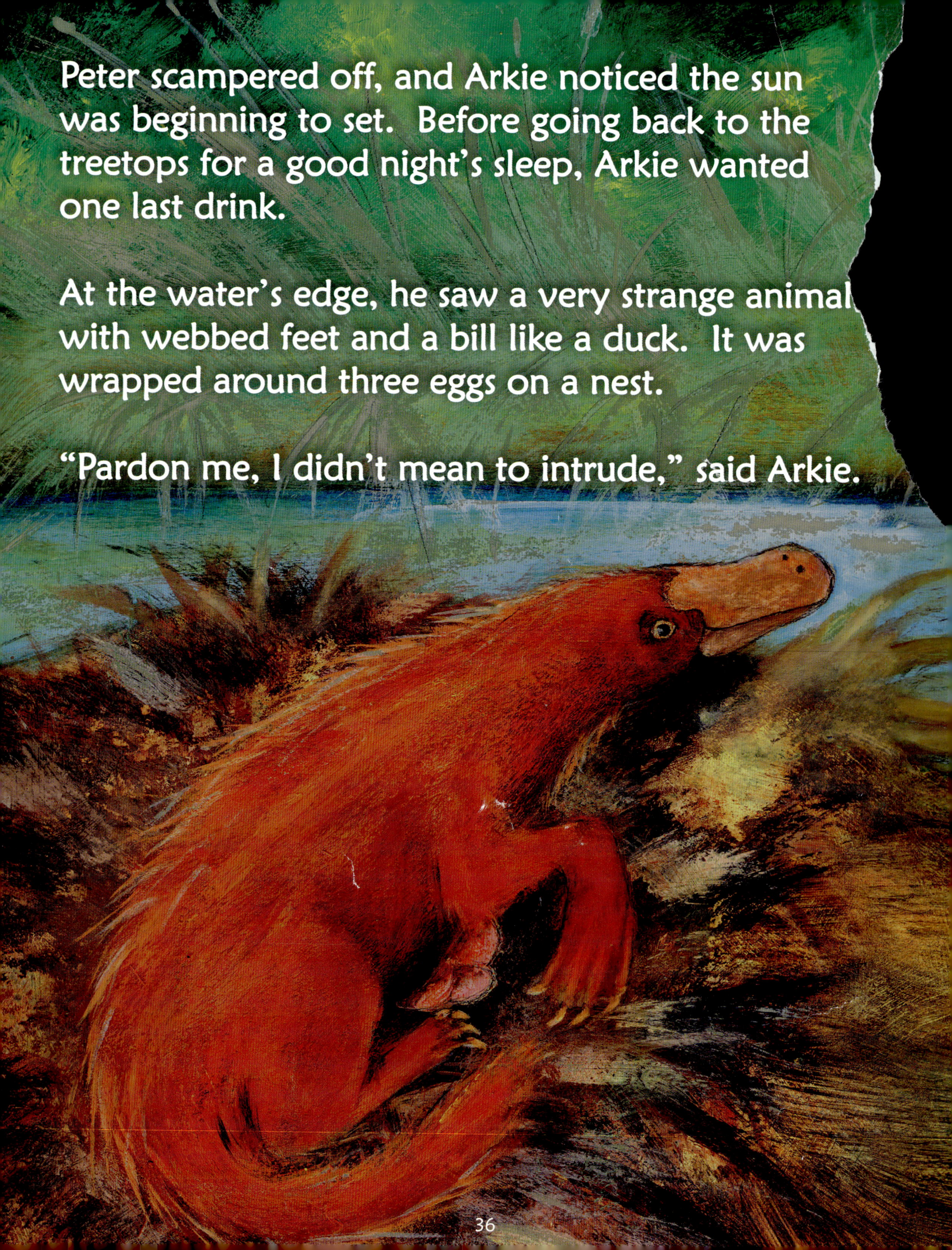

Peter scampered off, and Arkie noticed the sun was beginning to set. Before going back to the treetops for a good night's sleep, Arkie wanted one last drink.

At the water's edge, he saw a very strange animal with webbed feet and a bill like a duck. It was wrapped around three eggs on a nest.

"Pardon me, I didn't mean to intrude," said Arkie.

"That's okay. My name is Patty the platypus. Who are you?"

"I'm Arkie the archaeopteryx. I've never seen a platypus before. You lay eggs and build a nest like a bird," replied Arkie.

"Yes that's right, but I'm just another type of mammal. Well, if you don't mind, I have to get back to minding these eggs."

"Of course. Have a good night, Patty."

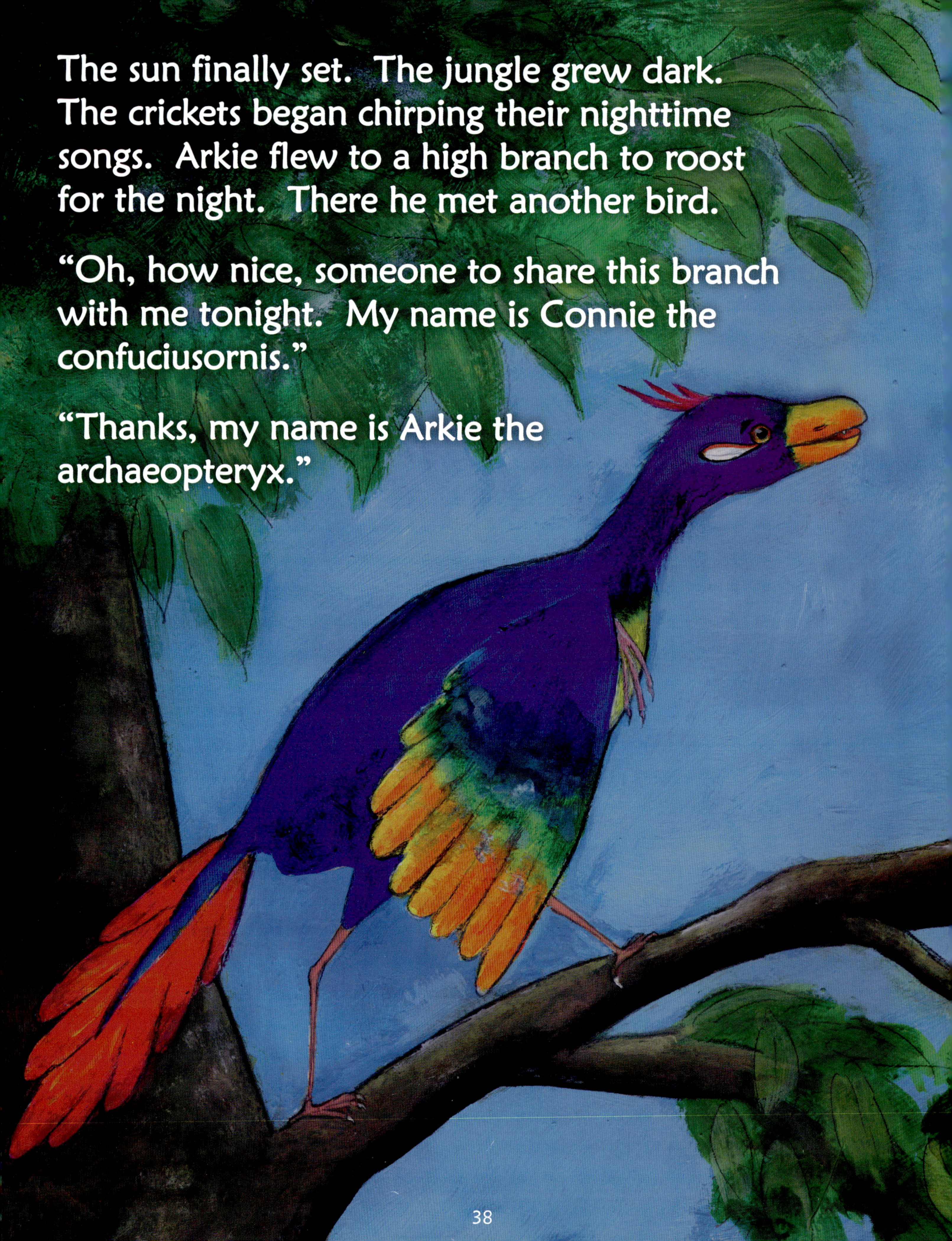

The sun finally set. The jungle grew dark. The crickets began chirping their nighttime songs. Arkie flew to a high branch to roost for the night. There he met another bird.

“Oh, how nice, someone to share this branch with me tonight. My name is Connie the confuciusornis.”

“Thanks, my name is Arkie the archaeopteryx.”

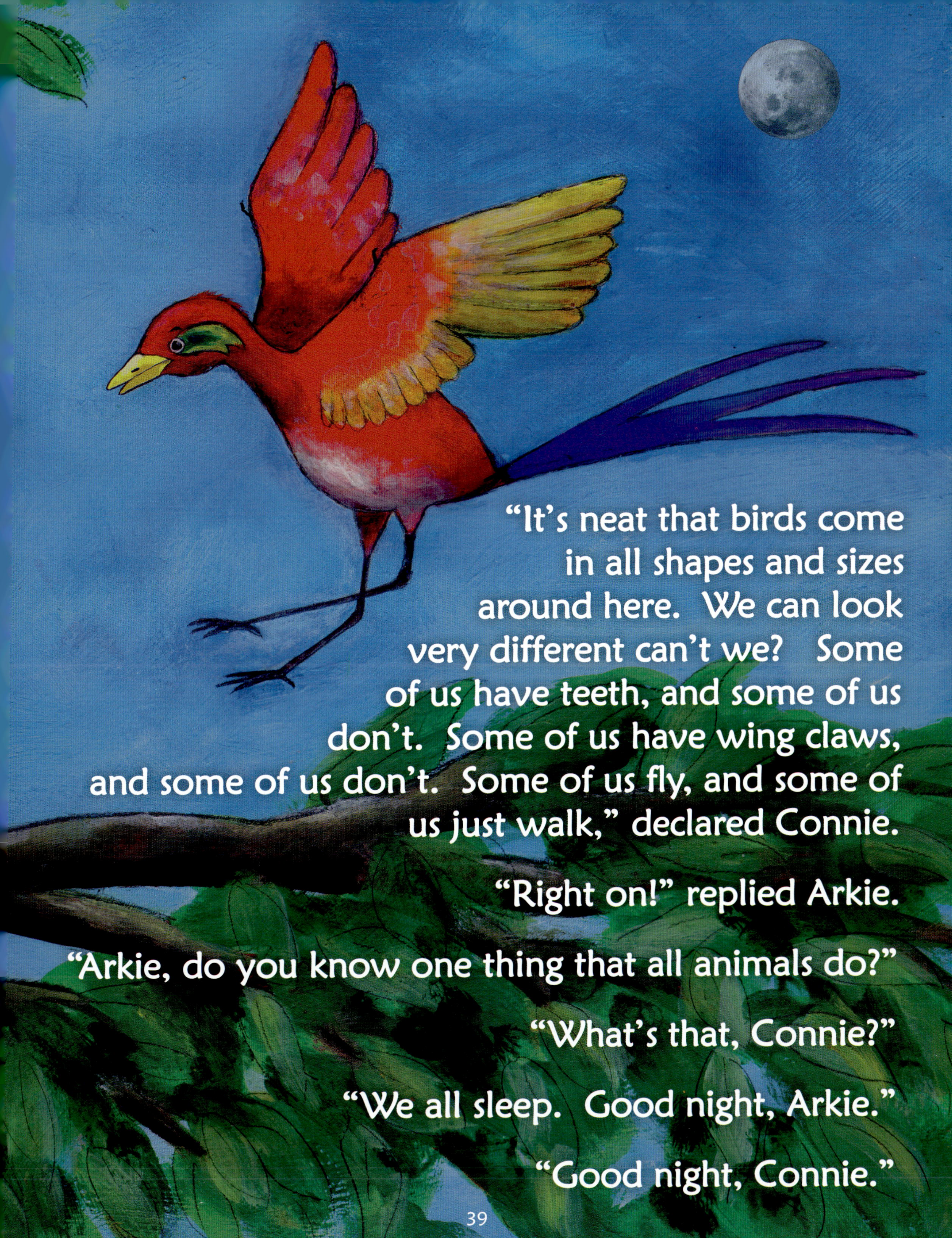

"It's neat that birds come in all shapes and sizes around here. We can look very different can't we? Some of us have teeth, and some of us don't. Some of us have wing claws, and some of us don't. Some of us fly, and some of us just walk," declared Connie.

"Right on!" replied Arkie.

"Arkie, do you know one thing that all animals do?"

"What's that, Connie?"

"We all sleep. Good night, Arkie."

"Good night, Connie."

Arkie drifted off to sleep on the high branch under the sparkling stars and dreamed about all the new friends he had met that day. Hank, a walking fish. Laura, a furry lobster. Alex, an axolotl who looked like a fish. Freddy, a frog with hair on its back. Leonard, a lizard without legs. Sino, a dinosaur with fuzzy skin on his back. Peter the pangolin, a scaly mammal. Patty the platypus, a bird-like mammal. And Connie the confuciusornis, a different kind of bird.

That day, Arkie learned that the Lord made some very unique creatures that defy man-made classification. He also learned that unrelated animals can share similar features, because they are all made by the same designer ...

The Lord God
made them all!

The

end

About the author: Ryan Jaroncyk

Ryan Jaroncyk is a prolific creationist writer who works for *Creation Ministries International* in Atlanta, Georgia, USA. He has been married to his wife, Jackie, for three years and is passionate about presenting children with an intellectually stimulating and artistically exceptional perspective of biblical creation.

His late mother served as the inspiration in his calling to begin reaching children with this critical message.

About the artist: Lisa Sodera

Lisa is 22 years old and lives in the South of England. Her main areas of expertise are book design, filming and video editing.

An accomplished wildlife artist, Lisa works mainly with watercolour and acrylic on a variety of mediums including canvas. To see some of her work, visit www.onesmallmango.com.

Her main passions include being involved in her local church, cooking Indian food, and playing the piano.

About CMI

Creation Ministries International is a non-profit, non-denominational Christian ministry proclaiming the truth of the Bible. For over 30 years, we have provided real-world answers to the most-asked questions in the vital area of creation/evolution, where the Bible is most under attack today—Genesis.

Evolutionary beliefs are the most common basis given today for:

- Evading moral absolutes
- Denying the very existence of the biblical God
- Rejecting the authority of Scripture and the claims of Christ in general

Results show that demonstrating the Bible is grounded in real history strengthens Christians, motivating them to reach out to others, confident that the Bible can be trusted.

www.CreationOnTheWeb.com / .org